Simple Steps to Sales Success
By
Stephen Atkinson

Table of Contents

Introduction

Throughout this guide I will be outlining the strategies that will enable you to define your future sales success - whatever you want to achieve in your career, the Simple Steps will help you get there.

Salespeople are some of the best-paid individuals in the world, and often salespeople are paid for their practical knowledge and what they can do, rather than what it says they know or can do on paper. What this guide will do is help you join the ranks of those successful salespeople by giving you key knowledge that you can immediately put into practice.

What separates the average salesperson from a top salesperson? - The choices they make and the actions they take.

This guide shows you how to make the right choices and follow them up with positive action.

This guide is the sum of all my knowledge as a successful salesperson and salesperson manager, molded in one succinct guide. For many years I asked myself 'What makes a successful salesperson?' The answers I came up with directed the actions I took, the actions I took *caused* my salary to quadruple over a few short years - and throughout all this time I made notes on what worked and what didn't – some of these notes became the 'Simple Steps to Sales Success'. These steps worked for me and they can work for you too.

So welcome to the Simple Steps to Sales Success.

Throughout this guide we are going to breakdown into easy steps *exactly* what makes a successful sales person – from what abilities and attributes you need, to the key strategies when face-to-face with customers. But nothing comes for free, so there will be work required to master the Simple Steps; some will take longer to master than others, but these will represent *giant leaps* in your progress to becoming a great salesperson.

'It does not matter how slowly you go, so long as you do not stop.'
- Confucius

In every life there are opportunities. Opportunities to provide service; opportunities to build our confidence and self-image; opportunities to raise our standard of living; opportunities to enjoy our work. But just because life abounds with opportunities doesn't mean to say it's a done deal! Otherwise, we would all be catching opportunities as easy as butterflies in a net and our lives would be a never-ending summer. Nevertheless, opportunities abound in this fast paced world we have been born into. Every day a new breakthrough in the realms of physics, chemistry or biology underlines the progress we are making, every week we understand a little more about what makes us tick and how we can move towards attaining our true potential. This guide is about making the most of your opportunities.

Throughout this guide you will acquire the knowledge to assert yourself in your chosen field of excellence. You will become confident in the knowledge that you are in control, and are not controlled.

The following steps explain the fundamentals of selling, whether you are new to sales, are in the process of considering it as a career (and so putting you on the path to excellence), or if you have been in sales some time... welcome, by purchasing this guide you have acknowledged your desire to further your career and more swiftly achieve your goals.

Throughout this guide you will find key strategies, ideas and methods to ensure your success in the sales field.

In the following pages there will be no blaming your boss, your targets or your customers for the path your career takes - you, and only you are in control.

The Right Mind-Set, Values, Beliefs and Goals

The following sections deal with one of the most important, if not *the* most important aspect of being a successful salesperson. Your mindset, attitude or simply the way you think. We are going to go through the fundamentals that you will need to exceed your expectations and reach your goals in sales. We are going to go through the basics here; the absolute 'must haves'. Thousands of books have been written about attitude and behavior, and there is a good reason for this - it is very, very important, so ignore this area at your peril.

Attitude or the Right Mind Set is what separates the winners from the losers. Which do you want to be? I thought so! Then read on...

Beliefs

We all have things we believe in, and often the beliefs we have can affect our behavior – either negatively or for the good. The thing is a belief doesn't necessarily need to be true , but is often something we choose to believe is true, or was told by our parents, teachers or the books we have read that it is true.

Don't believe me, then consider the question below:

Q: Where do Christmas presents come from?

A: Santa brings them for all good boys and girls

The above is a commonly held belief held by a lot of children in the western world (similar beliefs are held by children all over the globe). Why did we believe this? Easy, because our parents said it was true, our teachers backed them up and all our friends believed the same thing.

As we grow up we realize that adults (or our parents) don't really have all the answers and are not all-knowing. Often the answers they give are simply a product of their beliefs (an opinion). As we got older still, we would seek our answers in other ways, by consulting books, the Internet or our friends, etc. We no longer believed our parents were all-knowing.

So here's another question, did believing in Santa Claus affect our behavior at that time? – Absolutely. We believed that being good equaled getting more presents from Santa.

Do beliefs affect our behavior? Yes.

Beliefs change behavior. Change the belief (it is irrelevant whether the belief is 'true') and you change the behavior.

Beliefs can be empowering or disempowering, and if you hold any disempowering or negative beliefs they can hold you back. So it may be time to have a look at the beliefs you hold and decide if they are negative beliefs (holding you back) or positive beliefs (pushing you forward)?

If you do find you have any negative beliefs (an example might be "I'll never be any good at sales calls.") – Then you really need to switch them for more positive ones.

Before you can change any negative beliefs to positives, you may need to challenge your current negative beliefs...

Here's the 2 step process of how to change beliefs:
1. Break down negative beliefs
2. Build up positive beliefs

Negative beliefs can hold you back... but why let them!

The easiest way to change your beliefs from negative to positive is to dismantle negative beliefs by asking yourself challenging questions...

Such as: If other salespeople hit their targets, then there must be a way for me to do similar?

Or

If sales techniques can be taught, can I learn the skills I need to progress?

Asking these types of questions of yourself and taking note of the common sense answers you come up with will start to destabilize your negative beliefs.

Once you have destabilized any negative beliefs by asking challenging questions, you need to build positive beliefs to replace them, again by asking questions.

Here are some examples:

What attributes do I currently possess that I can positively use to make more sales on a daily basis?

Or

What have a done in the past, that got me a great result, and can I use that knowledge to push me forward now?

Dismantling any negative beliefs you may have and replacing them with positive ones is not always easy, but it can be done by asking the right challenging questions.

What are the beliefs in your life, write them down, do you see any of them conflicting with your long term goals?

If so, consider breaking down the negative beliefs and replacing them with more positive ones.

Values

Values effectively define who we are. A value is simply a concept that at our most basic level means a great deal to us. Most people have an internal list of values; they could include Security, Respect, Love, Fun or Fitness for example.

When our life is in balance with our values we feel more fulfilled.

So if a person has the above values they may feel more fulfilled when they earn a good, steady wage, have their own house, have the respect of their friends and colleagues, a spouse that loves them, the opportunity to have fun, and the time to maintain their fitness.

So what has all of this got to do with successful sales - everything.

If you have some values which conflict with your success in sales, then you need to do one of three things, change your career, change the value or integrate the two - otherwise you are unlikely to be fulfilled (successful). Now you may be thinking, hang on, if my values are the things most important to me why should I want to change them. It's a good question, well, for instance, one of your values might be relaxation, you like nothing better than taking it easy, watching sport on TV, soaking up rays on the beach, etc. I'm not saying that this value is good or bad, right or wrong - but if this is one of your highest values that you 'value' above anything else - it will impede your chances of success. You will have a conflict of

10

interest; you cannot make a success of anything without putting the work in. This doesn't mean you have to ditch relaxation completely from your list of values, but it may mean you have to relegate it down the list of importance - in other words, there will still be time in your world for being very relaxed, and you will enjoy it just the same as you did before, but it won't be so important in your life. What are the values in your life, write them down, do you see any of them conflicting with what you are trying to achieve?

Goals

Here we are going to define the basics of goal setting. In sales, this is usually pretty easy as you are often targeted to draw in a certain amount of business, or sign up more customers, or sell a certain number of widgets. This is great - you are given a goal and date by which to achieve it. On top of this you are likely to given the tools to achieve it: possibly a list of prospects or target groups, new literature/samples and a marketing/sales strategy to follow. Basically, in this example, your path has been shown to you and you simply follow it.

Golden Rule #1: If it isn't moving you towards your goal, why are you doing it?

If you haven't been clearly shown what your goals are and how to achieve them, you need to set them yourself, following this 4 step process:

1. Define what you want to achieve (your goal)
2. Define where you are right now (your starting point)
3. Draw up a plan that will take you there

4. Follow the plan*

* If the plan doesn't appear to be working, then adjust the plan and continue towards your goal.

You may say, well I'm not used to setting my own goals; I work on commission, the more I sell the more I earn. That's good, but it isn't a goal, it's too 'fuzzy'. You must define exactly how much commission you wish to earn, and then work out how many widgets/new customers you will bring on board to achieve that commission.

Don't aim too low, setting a goal to achieve the same amount of commission/bonus as last year isn't a goal, it's almost a certainty, especially if you keep on doing exactly what you did last year!

Goals need to stretch you, don't be afraid of setting them too high. Falling short of a high goal (e.g. Coming in 41% over target instead of 45%) is still a great result, falling short of a low goal can be a disaster (e.g. Coming in 2% under target instead of 2% above it). Aim high and go for it - what have you got to lose?

What about the plan? I hear you say!

You know where you want to go; you know where you are now. But how to get from here to there?

The key thing here is to totally focus on the goal, the plan will come, believe me, but the main thing is to take a positive step towards the goal. This means doing something positive in the pursuit of your goal, not just 'thinking' about anything. A positive something, might be setting time aside right away to analyze your customer base, to see who isn't buying your new widget, and calling them to set up appointments. Keeping your goal in mind and taking positive physical steps towards it will help you formulate an overall plan for achieving the goal.

'I have learned that if one advances confidently in the direction of his dreams, and endeavors to live the life he has imagined, he will meet with a success unexpected in common hours.' - Henry David Thoreau

What if some of the steps that formulate your plan don't appear to be working? That's OK, the main thing is that you have noticed they're not working and now you can do something about it. You should always be aware of the results of any actions or steps you take on your plan to achieve your goal. After every step, ask yourself this question: Has this action moved me closer toward my goal, Y/N? If the answer is Yes, all good and well, if it is No, then analyze why it didn't move you closer to your goal and seriously consider changing part of your plan (this could be a small change or a big change - but it does not necessarily mean changing your whole plan, and it certainly doesn't mean giving up).

During the execution of your plan, you may need to alter your course several times to 'navigate' to your desired goal. Every adjustment in direction will give you more information on how best to reach your objective, and you can adjust your plan correspondingly.

Very few people who set out to achieve a goal know how to get there when they set out - if they did then everyone would be achieving their goals. Successful goal-setters often set out in the direction of their goal and then they notice that maybe they are not getting any closer to it (some people call this making a mistake; that's fine, we all make them - the key is to notice when we've made them and do something about it) and they change direction by adjusting something they are doing so they are heading back in the direction of their goal - like a yacht 'tacking' towards the harbor into a head wind.

Keep your goal in focus and change your plan as required and you will achieve your goal.

You can adjust your plan, but your goal doesn't change.

Focus

Focus and concentration also have a part to play in maintaining the successful salesperson's attitude. Concentrated action will always pay dividends. If you encounter a problem bring all your concentration to bear to ensure a positive outcome.

Concentrate on the now, the present. Focusing on the past will get you nowhere; if I'd done this? If I done that? - Is a waste of time. The past is gone it cannot be changed and dwelling on any past mistake or regrets will keep you focused on the past

Concentrate on the present. Concentrating on the future often takes the form of worrying, what if this happens? What if they don't like me? – Your future depends upon the actions you take in the present, so plan your future in the present, live in the present, focus in the present.

Focus is especially important when it comes to customers. Everyone likes to feel important and respected; make sure that in your daily interactions with your customers, you focus only on them; don't rush them, don't tell them you need to be somewhere else, make sure that you are concentrating entirely on their needs or issues – only make promises when you know you can keep them, and when you do make them, ensure that you keep them – that is customer focus.

The Extra Mile

This is an 'Oldie', but a 'Goldie'. Going the extra mile, that is doing more than is expected of you, will build your customer loyalty faster than you ever dreamed possible.

But, why go the extra mile, don't you already work hard enough as it is? You need to go the extra mile now so you don't have to run extra miles later (then you really will be working hard!).

'A superior man is modest in his speech, but exceeds in his actions.' - Confucius

Here is an example of what I mean.

A customer asks you about a product that you do not supply and which is not in competition with your range of products. You have a vague idea of the product and the company, but simply tell your customer you don't supply that type of product and leave it at that – your customer will think no less of you. The next time you meet your customer, ask yourself: has your relationship/bond with that customer moved on?

No, not really!

Or you could do this...

When your customer asks about this product, you tell him that you don't supply that type of product, but if he wishes, you will try and find out who supplies it and maybe try and get the salesperson's name, then follow through on your promised action (see section on Focus). Your customer will think no less of you, in fact, he will feel the complete opposite, this action (which is of no material benefit to yourself) will greatly enhance your credibility in the eyes of the customer, taking you one step closer to being a trusted product advisor than a mere salesperson. Has your relationship/bond with this customer moved on?

You bet it has!

Find an opportunity to go the extra mile and your credibility (and therefore your sales will rocket).

The great thing about taking the second course of action is that you cannot lose. If, for example, you get nowhere finding out about the product, that's fine – call up your customer and simply tell him, he will appreciate your openness and the fact that you tried, and that will stand you in good stead on your next visit. If you do find out about the product and give him a call with the salesperson's name – then all to the good, you both win – and your customer will be grateful to you for helping him out. Even if you put him in touch with the other company and they 'blow it' by not answering his calls, or providing a poor service or product, this will only reflect badly on them – not on you or your company, after all you helped him, and it certainly isn't your fault that another company didn't follow though – you tried your best, you went the extra mile, and that is what he will remember.

Golden Rule #2: Never tell a customer "That isn't my job."

Learn from Others

In sales there is no need to reinvent the wheel. Let your manager know what you want to do and why, then find out in your team who is the top player (this shouldn't be difficult), don't be proud, ask them how they managed to outsell the rest of the team by X percent. Tell them you want to do the same - in 99 cases out of a hundred they will be flattered and tell you - follow their advice (as long as it's ethical and legal). Salespeople are competitive by nature, but when they are at the top of their game they are rarely concerned about giving away their tips.

Team Player

Ensure that you integrate into your sales team and wider circle of colleagues. As with section above, be open and honest with your colleagues and show mutual respect to them all (and mean it), even when you don't agree with their viewpoints or even particularly like some of them. Within all teams there will be subgroups of people, team members whose share interests or viewpoints or simply started at the same time and trained together (strong bonds are often formed between individuals when they are training together for a certain period of time - these bonds can often last a lifetime).

The formation of like-minded sub groups within teams is natural and rarely causes any problems, however, if there happens to be a group of individuals with a collective and negative mindset, avoid, at all costs becoming one of them or even being associated with them. Aligning yourself with a negative group will do two things: 1) Start influencing your attitude from positive to negative, and 2) Draw attention to the fact that you are associating with the 'Nay Sayers', and everyone knows they are negative and so does your boss - if you want to be a winner this is definitely not the way to do it. Do the opposite, ensure that you associate with the 'positives' - they will encourage you, and lift you - and they won't drain your energy.

Treat everyone else in the organization with the same respect from the office junior to the CEO. Everyone's job is important to the organization and the people around you will in turn like you, respect you and your opinion - and ultimately help you rise through the ranks.

When you are a team player, remember that at all times you have opportunities to shine or fade into the background - ensure that you shine - always - even when you think no-one is looking - especially at sales conferences/trade shows etc.

Golden Rule #3: Never undermine person's position (job)

Accentuate the Positive

In a nutshell, this means look for the good in everything and everyone. It does not mean playing 'Pollyanna' or being a 'Yes' man (or woman), it simply means that when a 'problem' arrives on your doorstep treat it has one side of a coin, the other being the solution - your job is 'guess' (work out) the solution. One of the ways of doing this might be to think of the complete opposite of the problem, the 'anti-problem'? That then becomes your goal, and the solution is the route you take to it.

Problem - Solution - Goal

Here's an example.

What's the problem: Widget No. 3 sales have dropped below your target this month for you, but the rest of the sales team seems to be growing theirs.

What's the opposite of the Problem: Widget No 3 sales above target next month (you obviously can't change the result for this month, unless you have a time machine). Solution(s): Explore why some sales people are up, what are they doing differently from you, is one target group of customer buying more than another, and is there a seasonal/geographical reason for the slump. What are you doing that is working, define it and do more of it. What are you doing that isn't working - stop doing it. Keep focused on the goal and change your approach when you have gathered your information. Be solution focused, not problem focused.

Accentuate the positive when things don't work out, when things go wrong - when you get an unexpected (bad) result. Every action you take (or fail to take) generates a result - cause and effect.

Do not see what could be perceived as 'poor' results as 'failure'; every time you generate a 'failure' result, it takes you one step closer to your 'success' result. Every so called 'failure' is a waving flag trying to get your attention; 'Hey, look at me, I'm not exactly what you hoped for, but if you ask the right questions I'll point you towards your goal!'. When you get a result you didn't want or expect you need to ask yourself one key question (and it isn't 'why does this always happen to me?') - The key question you need to ask is: What does this result teach me? And when you have explored all the answers to that question, ask: How can I use what I've learned from this result to take me further towards my goal? When you have an answer to the questions, adjust your approach and continue towards your goal.

In being positive, the rule with people is easy: If you haven't got anything good to say about someone, then say nothing at all (by the way if you look hard enough you will always find something to like).

Think Win/Win

We'll go into this in more detail, but the basis of Win/Win is that if you always try to achieve Win/Win you will never be seen as weak or manipulative by your customers or colleagues, and that again will reflect positively in your sales.

Be a Winner!

Being a winner in sales is what you want to be right? Otherwise, you wouldn't be reading this book would you?

20

To be a winner in sales you need to combine all the attributes discussed in this section which cumulatively add up to the winning attitude that will ultimately govern your actions and so your results. Thinking like a winner is key, but you must also look like a winner externally, this means dressing like a winner.

'Model' a winner in your organization or even a celebrity that exudes 'winner'. How do they dress? How do they speak? What does their body language say?

I'm not saying you have to 'mimic' or copy people and not be yourself, but by studying other 'winners' dress sense, speech patterns and physiology you will notice that there are some things 'winners' do that others don't - some of these winning 'traits' - you may want to adopt.

'Clothes make the man. Naked people have little or no influence on society.' - Mark Twain

Be aware of what works and what doesn't work and adopt your strategy accordingly.

Organizational Skills, Research and Planning

This next section focuses on the key organizational skills you will need to be a super successful sales person. There are many very successful sales people out there who are very disorganized, but these are a few and far between, they may be 'naturals', but they are rare and whose to say these gifted individuals couldn't be more successful if they were organized.

There are also some very, very organized sales people out there who are great... at organizing, but not at sales. These people tend to focus on the organizing and not the sales goal (target), so they achieve all their organizational goals, but not their sales targets!

Nether the less organizational skills are important.

The next few insights give you the core areas of organization skills that will improve your time/journey planning, decrease your stress levels, boost your confidence and improve your image with your customers and your boss.

'By failing to prepare, you are preparing to fail.' - Benjamin Franklin

Pre-call research

Knowledge is power (but only if you know what to do with it!). Before visiting any customer ensure you do your homework, this means finding out as much as you can about the customer whether they be an individual or an organization.

Again the web is a great place to start, especially in reference to companies, look for what their long term goals are, is there any way in which your product or service could move them closer to them?

What is the gossip on this customer?

Be very careful here because 'gossip' is simply someone's opinion (often distorted by repetition) and that is not the same as the truth, so anything you hear (positive or negative), take it on board, but take with a 'pinch of salt' - and certainly do not base your entire call around hearsay.

The same rules apply for customer records written by your predecessor; any records are only their opinion at that time. Just because they didn't get on with a customer doesn't mean that you can't and vice versa (although that won't happen if you want to be a successful sales person!).

Gaining Appointments

When calling by phone an appointment for a sales call over the phone, some simple rules apply, here they are:

Remember your only goal is to make an appointment to get in front of the customer/prospective customer. That's it!

Before you make any call reacquaint yourself with the customer's details/records and have them in front of you during the call.

Don't use a 'script' to read from, this can sound 'robotic' or 'lifeless', but certainly have a short list of 'points' you may want to mention.

During the conversation use simple uncomplicated words, pace the speed of your voice along with that of the customer, same goes for your tone.

Never use technical jargon, buzz words or swear.

Smile as you dial the last digit of the telephone number and enter into the conversation with an enthusiastic and friendly attitude.

Expect a positive outcome to the call - that is the achievement of your goal.

Tell them your name and what you do: Do this very briefly and right at the beginning of the conversation.

Use referrals: If you have them, use them. E.g. "Jim Fraser at Fraser Foods suggested you might be interested in our product/service..."

Ask if they have a couple of minutes to talk - if they have, don't ramble on for an hour

Give them a broad and very brief benefit of your product, followed immediately by a qualifying question. E.g. "Our new service is proven to save our customers money, is that an area you are interested in?"

Do not try to 'sell' your service/product over the phone, if the customer gives positive answers to a couple of questions like the one above, then suggest that you met up

Give the customer options. E.g. Ask "When is the most convenient time for you, I can make next Tuesday morning or Thursday the 17th in the afternoon?" - This type of question does several things, it ensures you are leading the conversation, it subconsciously lets the customer know that you are organized and that your time as well as theirs is valuable. By giving them options to choose from, you give the customer something solid to focus on, they simply look in their diary and decide which one of the options is better and 9 times out of 10 will ask you to come in on that day. Even if both the options turn out to be no good you have got the customer thinking seriously about the appointment, so give them another couple of options to choose from or ask them the day that would suit them best, but don't accept their suggestion if it is in the next day or two, this will undue all their perceptions of you keeping a full and organized diary.

Tell the customer you are putting the date in your diary right now and reiterate when you will see them. This will prompt them to do similar.

Pre-call Planning

One of the easiest ways pre-plan your call is to use visualization. This is easy to do and it doesn't have to be perfect every time.

For visualization to help in your pre call planning, you need to imagine the call from start to finish and mentally note any aspects of the call that would cause you problems in a achieving your goal of a successful sales call.

You need to do a minimum of a couple of visualizations on this to ensure you get the best out of it. But, don't worry visualizing a call is not done in real time, so you should be able to visualize the entire call in 30 seconds to 2 minutes - this is time well spent.

Here's how you do it...

Close your eyes and imagine yourself preparing to set off for your appointment. You consult your road map to ensure you know the way (mental note: Have you a road map?). The first half of the journey takes you along a road you know well, imagine this in detail, some of the road signs, those road works that seem to have been in place for months(mental note: set off slightly early to ensure on time). You arrive at the customer premises with a little time to spare, you use this time to re-read your customer notes/product literature (mental note: Take relevant notes and product literature). You next see yourself being shown into the customer's office and after some pleasantries begin the sales interview in earnest. Imagine some the questions the customer might ask you (do you know all the answers? If not, make a mental note to brush up on them). The customer asks to see a sample of the product and later some testimonials (mental note ensure you have the relevant samples and testimonials). You see the call going well throughout and in the end the call the customer placing an order (mental note: have you the necessary order forms/details) or agreeing the next stage in the buying process. Imagine yourself shaking hands with the customer and leaving their office.

OK, that's visualization one, now write down all your mental notes before you forget them:

Road Map

Early Start

Notes and literature

Answers to obvious questions

Samples and testimonials

Ordering forms/details

Take action on all the points of the above list and ensure you have them all covered before doing the call for real.

A second visualization is often useful in a similar vain to the one above, but this should be even slicker, as you won't need to 'pause' to make mental notes (having ensured the potential glitches don't occur), this one should go smoothly and without a hitch culminating in you achieving your goal. The best time to do this second visualization is just before the call for real. Arrive a little early, and when you safely parked the car, close your eyes for a minute and run through this second visualization - it goes without saying do not attempt to do visualizations whilst driving, operating machinery etc.

Finding your Way!

Or route planning, as it is also known is a relatively easy concept to grasp, and although there are several systems that are commonly used (your company may have one in place now), territory route planning boils down to a few simple basics:

Plan ahead: Ensure you know where you are going each day, well in advance and allow enough time to get between appointments. This seems obvious, but it is surprising how often a poor (in both senses of the word) salesperson steps out of the front door in the morning with only the vaguest idea of where they are going – you can imagine how much this impresses their manager!

Be prepared: Stuff happens, be ready for it. If it's winter, ensure you allocate enough time at the start of the day to clear the snow off the car should the temperature drop. If it's summer, anticipate the holiday traffic, what is your back up plan if you can't make that next appointment in time (see below).

Give 'options' when booking appointments

'Cluster' calls in the same geographical area to minimize driving time/maximize customer time

Use 'Down-time' (arriving early for appointments, waiting on delays, coffee breaks) to review literature and make plans

Prioritize calls: This is important. You should prioritize your calls by how much they will positively or negatively affect your target. What do I mean? Here's an example: You will have 4 calls to make tomorrow at: 1)10am, 2)12 noon, 3)2.30pm and 4)4pm. The first call (1) is to see a good customer who has been encountering some problems with your company/product, you need to sort the problems out or you could lose business. Call number 2 is to a new prospect, and the call is basically to find out who they are and what the potential is. Call number 3 is to seal a deal you have been working on for some months and could potentially win you some good business. Call number 4 is a good prospect, has shown interest but so far hasn't committed to buying. This is how you should prioritize these customer calls using the 'bottom line rule'.

Call 1: Top priority, call on at all costs, it will be hard to win this customer back should you lose him, and losing him even for a short time will negatively affect your chances of hitting your target.

Call 3: This is your second priority, this appointment can positively affect your chances of hitting target, earning you more bonus.

Call 4: This call is your third priority, potential business but not yet in the bag (don't get carried away, a Maybe can be a long way from a Yes).

Call 2: This call is the least important of the day, the potential customer isn't earning you any bonus, and you don't know what the potential is, it could be good or it could be bad - so you need to favor the calls with guaranteed potential over this one.

Prioritizing your Time

Prioritizing your most valuable commodity - Time!

Fundamental Truths

    You can't manage time (It will flow 24/7)
    You can only manage yourself

Planning your time well and setting your priorities is a habit worth cultivating. This means deciding:

In which order tasks should be handled?

How much time should be allocated to each task?

The most common mistake when planning your time and prioritizing your tasks is...

... Not distinguishing between urgent and important tasks.

Urgent Tasks

Don't always have the highest payoff

Often get priority over important tasks

Often unplanned

Always time-bound

Important Tasks

Are the ones that help us achieve our overall purpose

Golden Rule #4: The more you focus your time, energy and overall planning on the important tasks, the less time you will need to spend on urgent tasks.

Urgent tasks may be urgent and some will also be important - but try to minimize the urgent tasks by focusing on the important and planning your time well. If you are continually focusing on the urgent, you are doing a lot of unnecessary fire-fighting, and consistent fire-fighting will burn you out...

Controlling the Controllable

You can't do everything

A sales career can often be a frustrating arena, especially to the uninitiated and when things go wrong. As a successful salesperson you need to be cool, calm and collected under pressure. Along with planning your journeys and prioritizing your work as in the above two sections, you need to realize one thing - sometimes things are out of your control; trying to gain control over something which is clearly out of your control is called worrying, and worrying will get you nowhere fast.

Golden Rule #5: Control the controllable.

You won't be too long into your sales career, when, if you care (and you obviously do) you will want 'to do' everything: Make your product, package it, market it, pick and pack it, deliver it and invoice it. You will then want to ensure that all queries or complaints are promptly dealt with and your customer is absolutely and totally delighted with your product or service.

But you can't do all the above things, because you have the big job - you have to sell it. To sell the product/service you need to maintain focus and not get sidetracked by all the things that might or could go wrong. Every time you feel that you might be getting sidetracked ask yourself this question: "Is this moving me closer towards achieving my target?", if the answer is no then you need to get back on track pronto! Apart from being sidetracked by wanting to do everything yourself, if you are not careful you can be sidetracked by other people - remember other peoples' priorities are not yours - so sometimes you will have to say No.

Golden Rule #6: Never 'blame' your colleagues for something going wrong, when you are with your customer

You can't do all the things yourself just to make sure everything goes right for the customer. But you can help. There will be people in your organization that are 'doers', they say they will do something and they do it. Unfortunately, there will be some people in your organization that are the complete opposite - 'coasters' - if you have to work with people who are unreliable, here's a way to deal with them - Let them set their own deadlines, make a note of the deadline they say and chase them immediately they don't meet it. This is fair, it lets them choose their own deadline, but they will quickly realize that you aren't going to let them forget about it - once you've done this a couple of times they are less likely to let you down.

Product Knowledge, Features versus Benefits

I'll say it again, knowledge is power – but only if you know how to use it. As a successful salesperson you need to know your product very well. You'll notice I say very well, and not inside out – inside out is not usually necessary, but knowing your product very well is fundamental if you want to succeed.

Getting to Know Your Products

It is imperative that you and your product/service(s) get on friendly terms; this doesn't mean that if you have several products in your 'bag' that you need to know all the different size/color/product codes by heart.

Golden Rule #7: If you can easily look it up, don't bother trying to memorize it

'Friendly terms' means you are comfortable and confident when speaking about your product. This is very important when you are in front of customers; if you don't feel 'comfortable' with a product it will show – and they won't buy. They won't buy because it's too fiddly, it's too difficult to get out of the packaging, the instructions are too vague, there is too much to remember – and if the salesperson couldn't use it properly what chance do they have!

Get comfortable, get confident. When you are trained on the use of your product/service, be the one to ask all the 'dumb' questions (these are the ones that will crop up first when you are out in the field), be attentive and interested (no matter what the reactions of your peers are!), read all the supporting literature you are given especially that which is intended for your customers.

Use 'dead time', that is any time where you find you have a few spare minutes to kill (e.g. An appointment in the middle of the day may have been cancelled) to read through relevant literature pertaining to your product/service – it is amazing how you can enhance your knowledge in this way.

If you can, and it is safe and ethical to do so, test the products yourself, this way you can anticipate any possible drawbacks the customer may come up with and also you may discover added benefits (so if you sell toothbrushes – brush your teeth with your product, if you sell pens make sure you write with yours etc.). Some products, it goes without saying, you won't be able to test yourself (because they are unsuitable or dangerous, etc.) such as surgical knee replacements or dog worming tablets or any pharmaceutical products.

Getting to the Heart of Things

All products have features, but they are sold by focusing the customer's attention on the benefit that a feature gives.

Please read that line again. Get this one wrong and you lose the sale.

For those new to sales. A feature tends to be a physical aspect of a product or service, here's a couple of examples:

'The new RolloPen from Wonder Pens incorporates a stainless steel casing (feature), rendering this stylish new ballpoint almost indestructible and so promises years of reliable use (benefit).'

'Silver Guardian Alarms' 24/7 advice line (feature) means help is only a phone call away, ensuring guaranteed continuity of security (benefit).'

Golden Rule #8: Say the feature, play the benefit

In getting to know your products you need to know what the features of your product are, what is the advantage of any particular feature and what's the benefit to the customer.

This is getting to the heart of things.

If the customer does not see the benefit in a product he or she will not buy.

It is often easy to get carried away with the features of particular products (this happens a lot with new, innovative products, gadgets, computer software and hardware) without explaining the corresponding benefit and therefore losing the sale.

It is no use explaining that your product has a Super-Duper Thermal Iso-Shield of expanded poly-whatsits, if you don't go on to explain that this feature increases insulation and therefore will keep their sandwiches cold.

The next time you go into a store and the salesman is explaining the merits of the latest gizmo to you, consciously check if they are trying to sell the features when they should be selling the benefits!

List some of the features of your product and the corresponding benefits.

The Word on the Street...

When promoting your product or service you may be given all sorts of backup to 'prove' the benefits your product or service can deliver. And whilst it is important, as we have discussed, to know your product well; it is equally important to know what your customers (current users) are saying about your product.

Golden Rule #9: In the world of sales - perception is everything

How do the current customers perceive your product/service and does their perception match with the official version (e.g. the claims your sales literature makes?). Knowing what your current customers think of your product now, can help you sell it to more customers in the future - if they really like your product, you might ask them for a 'third party reference', this could be a powerful tool in promoting your product.

Don't forget to ask your current users what they think is the best benefit of your product (you may be surprised) and concentrate on that benefit in future calls - after all if they like, there is a good chance someone else will.

The Story of a Successful Sales Call

The successful sales call is at the core of a successful career in sales. It is what happens when a salesperson meets with a customer that defines their level of success in sales. The next few sections concentrate on this key process, breaking it down into manageable and logical steps.

You will see the importance of preparation, presentation and first impressions.

The sales call can be likened to a good story, and as with all good stories it needs to have a beginning, a middle and an end - and you as the author of this story, having done your research in advance (after all your story needs to stand up to scrutiny) need to ensure a happy ending.

Prologue to a Sales call

Before any successful sales call, as we have discussed in the previous sections, you need to be prepared.

Here's a checklist of what you should know before you start the call. Are you prepared?

The customer's history?

Info from previous sales person's records (if appropriate)?

Who's who in the organization?

Anticipated questions?

What your goal for this call is?

Have you all the correct paperwork/samples?

The Successful Sales Call: In the beginning…

The core of a successful sales call is more often than not simply asking the right questions - but before you seriously get into the sales call you need to set the scene. This part of the call is vitally important if you are to make the right (professional) impression and ensure that you have the best chance of achieving your goal for this call.

This part of the call needs total clarity, and because of that it is often best kept very, very simple.

Here's how it breaks down:

Tell them <u>who</u> you are and simply <u>why</u> you are there

Back that up with <u>what</u> this might mean for them (keep it broad and general)

Get the <u>'Thumbs Up'</u> to move on to the rest of the call

Who - Why - What - Thumbs Up?

Here how it might sound in real life:

"Good Morning, My Name is Jerry Cornelius from Super Secure Alarms (Who). And I'm here to give you an insight into our new range of security products (Why), which I believe can help enhance your company's security and safeguard its people and its assets (What). But before *you* can assess whether Super Secure Alarms can assist you in meeting your security needs, I'd like to ask a few questions to help me better understand your requirements. Is that OK? (Thumbs Up?)"

You can obviously develop your own version of this introduction to suit your product, your audience or your personality. But remember to include all the elements: Who, Why, What and Thumbs Up - this will give you the best chance of 'getting off on the right foot', and not making the error of getting halfway through the call before your customer lets you know he has no idea why you are there and or indeed, who you are (trust me on this, I've seen it happen).

Listen Up!

The ability to ask good questions lies at the absolute core of any good sales call. This is coupled with the ability to listen. For most people listening well does not come naturally; it has to be practiced. You can ask the greatest questions in the world, but if you are not 'really listening' to the answers they produce then they are all in vain. Listening is a skill, it can be learnt. Practice it.

Listening should not be passive when you are talking to your customer (it is not like listening to the radio, where the sound can simply wash over you almost unnoticed). You need to summon all your concentration to listen well to your customer, and they need to know that you are listening well. Letting your customer know that you are listening to them is easy to do, but again may take some practice until it becomes a positive habit. Here are the key things that will let your customer know you are listening:

Maintain good eye contact: The does not mean 'staring your customer out', as prolonged, unbroken eye contact will eventually make them very nervous (not good and not funny). Good eye contact simply means looking your customer in the eye, especially when they or you are speaking, natural breaks in eye contact are absolutely fine, indeed involuntary eye movements will happen, for example, when you are recalling something or considering a problem (but that's the subject for another book). The main thing is that if you are looking them in the eye, they will think, and rightly so, that all your attention is focused on them. Letting yourself be distracted, even for a second, by, for instance glancing out of the window or at your watch, is likely to break the rapport you have been establishing with the customer, which in turn will have a negative effect on your call. Keep focused on the customer.

Paraphrase the customer: This can seem a little awkward at first, but this is a very powerful way of letting the customer know you are listening. When the customer makes a particularly valid point, repeat it back to them in your own words:

"So, what you're saying Mr. Jones is that…"

This will let the customer know that you have been listening and that you understand what they are saying. It will also help embed this piece of information into your memory.

Ask the customer to repeat something: This shows the customer that you're listening and are seeking to understand their viewpoint fully. Only do this occasionally as appropriate during a call, doing it more than once or twice will have the opposite effect and the customer will think you are not being attentive at all.

Nod and make positive sounds: Occasionally during the call, nod your head, say 'yes, I see' or 'Uhm, that is interesting" or similar.

Mirror the customer's voice tone, speech patterns: This does not mean to say you mimic the customer's voice, it simply means that if the customer speaks slowly and you speak fast then you need to bring your speed closer to theirs.

Mirror the customer's body language: This, when done well can help build rapport very quickly, but again do not try to copy every movement or they will think you are trying to be 'funny'. But if the customer is leaning forward (usually a sign they are interested in the subject being discussed or product demonstrated) then you don't want to be slumping back in your chair!

Mastering the art of actively listening is not easy, but it is worth it.

To truly communicate with your customer (and at a basic level, that is all selling really is), you have to find out what is most important to them. Selling implies that you 'make' somebody buy something - however, human beings generally only do what they want to do and you cannot make them 'buy' anything. They will, however, have requirements or needs, and if some of their needs are matched by the benefits of your product/service then they are likely to buy of their own volition.

But as we all know customers rarely, if ever, just come out and tell you exactly what they want...

"I want an easy and foolproof alarm system, to cover 7 separate areas, 2 sensors in an area, with 3 separate keypads in the 'key access areas'. Access codes to change every Friday at 2pm. The control pads need to be maroon with our corporate logo embossed on them, and I need the whole system fitted and working by April the 14th."

... Of course there are occasionally exceptions. Very occasionally.

So a customer will have certain requirements or needs, if you can 'satisfy' those needs with your product or service, then the customer is more likely to buy.

So what are these needs and how do we find them?

You find needs by asking questions - that's it.

Once you've found a particular need, you simply match that need to the corresponding benefit of your product or service.

More about the type of questions you ask in a minute, but for the moment, lets concentrate on the most important need of all. This is a fundamental need of all human beings.

Never forget it. Here it is... The <u>need</u> to be understood.

And you match this particular need, not with a benefit that your product or service offers, but with a benefit that you offer...

<u>The ability to listen to, and understand your customer's point of view</u>

This is why it is so important to let the customer know they are being listened to.

OK, how do we find the rest of the customer's needs?

Easy, ask questions.

Next time you are in the position to compare one salesperson with another, watch which one asks the most questions and listens attentively - that one will be the most successful.

In life there are lots of questions one could ask: Loaded questions, leading questions, curious questions, irritating questions... etc, etc.

In sales you can make it much simpler. In sales you need to ask two basic types of question.

The first type of question is sometimes known as an 'open' question. Open questions tend to elicit free flowing answers which often unearth a lot of information.

Open questions tend to begin or include the words:

Who

Where

How

Why*

What

When

*'Why' tends to be used as a question to obtain more information, following on from a previously asked open question. Be cautious and don't use 'why' questions too often during a call, sometimes people are intimidated by 'why' questions and become defensive - especially if you don't know them very well (e.g. First contact).

Here are some examples of open questions:

"Where are the areas you are seeking to improve your security systems?"

"How have the current security systems affected you?"

"Can you tell me why that is important?"

Open questions, as mentioned earlier, are designed to elicit a 'stream' of information, from which you can start to 'pick up' the customer's needs.

What sort of 'open' questions might you use in a sales call, write a few down.

The second type of question is sometimes known as a 'closed' question. A closed question's main purpose is to get specific, definite answers. Most commonly they will elicit a Yes or No response, but it could also be a date or a number.

Closed questions tend to begin or include the words:

How many

Is

Here are some examples:

"How many sensors will you require?"
"Is that important?"

Closed questions and the answers they bring forth tend to be short and to the point.

The answers the above two questions might get could be:

"16."

"Yes, very."

Closed questions can also be used to qualify a statement, in other words, they can be used to check if something is true or important as in the second example above - "Is that important?"

What sort of 'closed' questions might you use in a sales call, write a few down.

A good and balanced sales call will incorporate both these types of questions. If you were to conduct a call using only open questions you would end up tying yourself and your customer in knots, and eventually your customer would lose patience and you would lose the sale. Constantly asking open questions is very, very irritating after a while; children in particular are very good at it. Next time you meet a three-year-old just watch how many open questions they ask! (What happens when... Why is the sky blue... But, why... What happens then... Why is that?).

Equally, using just closed questions can sound abrupt, aggressive and interrogative. Using only closed questions will not elicit background information, you are unlikely to discover many needs and your customer will feel stressed and under pressure - and you will leave them thinking you are a very pushy salesperson. This does not bode well for your future relationship.

One of the keys to a good call is to use a balance of the two types of questions, but as a general rule start off with a few, well thought out, open questions. Starting this way will enable you to get a 'feel' for your customer and they will be far more relaxed than if you immediately started with closed questions.

Using these two types of simple questions well and listening carefully to the answers will enable you to find the customers' needs.

Golden Rule #10: Never boast about your sales achievements to a customer, even unintentionally

So you now can successfully navigate through the sales call using a selection of open and closed questions, and listen carefully to the answers they elicit. So what about the customer's needs?

Needs are not just something that the customer likes, they are important to him. This importance will come out in the words that the customer uses, the tonality of their voice and their body language.

Here are some of the words a customer might use when something is important to them, in other words when they are telling you a need:

Important

Imperative

Need

Want, etc.

Here are a few examples:

"It is important that this new system is easy to use."

"It is imperative we have a 24 hour back-up to ensure there are no gaps in our security."

"I need a fool-proof system."

"What I want is a security code that changes when I want it to, whether that is weekly or monthly."

Often needs will emerge in response to an open question, and they can be accompanied by the customer, emphasizing the need in the tone of his voice (i.e. Becoming more serious or excited) and their body language (e.g. Leaning forward). Needs can sometimes be apparent in these circumstances, but it is often useful to check you have found a need by asking a qualifying (or checking) closed question such as:

"So you are looking for a fool-proof system?"

To which the answer would usually be a Yes or a No.

Once a customer has told you about one of their needs/requirements, make sure that you fully understand why this is important to them. Once you understand a customer's particular need completely it will be much easier to match the relevant benefit your product or service can provide. Once you do fully understand, you need to let them know you have been listening and you understand - do this by simply saying - "Yes, I understand" (or something similar) or paraphrasing a concise version of what they have just said back to them.

When you have done that, simply go on to describe the feature/benefit of your product/service which most closely 'matches' their need.

"Our new Secure 2407 system is backed up by a 24 hour technical hotline service, ensuring that any issues can be dealt with quickly and efficiently."

Good. But don't assume that the customer makes the connection between what they want (need) and what you have to offer (benefit). So you need to check that they see the connection and are happy with it, by using a suitable closed question.

"Does that meet your requirements?"

At this point the customer will usually give a positive or a negative response.

If they give a positive response, good you have found one of the customer's needs and matched it with a relevant benefit of your product.

If the customer gives a negative response, you may not have sufficiently understood your customer's requirement, so the best option would be to delve further into the reasons why they have responded negatively. Use an open question such as:

"What else would be needed to fulfill your requirements?"

The customer may have other needs which you will have to find out about if you want to help them, to do this you will need to ask another open question and start the questioning process again:

"Is there anything else which you feel is important to you...?"

Ask enough questions until you fully understand your customer, this will be apparent when you next describe a benefit of your product that fully matches their requirements - then they will know you have listened and understood.

You will have to continue asking Open/Closed questions and matching needs against benefits throughout the body of the call. However, you will notice that in most calls the customer will have one over-riding need or requirement which is far more important than the rest - if you can satisfy this need then you have a good chance of ending the call on a positive note.

Golden Rule #11: Never criticize the competition or their products

A Happy Ending and Closing the Call

The next phase of the call is closing the call; there are many, many variations on closing a call from walking away with an order in your hand to simply agreeing with the customer what you need to do next.

If you have prepared well, listened to the customer, understood their point of view, matched their needs/requirements with the benefits your product can provide... then the next step, closing the call, should fall into place. If you have done the above steps well, then the close should 'evolve' naturally. This often means the customer will ask you what to do next or how do they go about buying this product.

If the close seems awkward, or ill timed then it is likely you have rushed the middle phase of the call or have simply not been listening to the customer.

If the call doesn't 'evolve' where the customer naturally takes the lead, but you believe you have discovered the customers needs and matched them accurately against your products' benefits then it is time for you to close the call.

The simplest and most straightforward way to close the call is to do a final review of all the pertinent points discussed, including any promises of further information, any information you will be sending through, but most importantly of all a review of the benefits of your product that have matched the customer's needs or requirements.

At this point do not be tempted to oversell your products by telling the customer about 'some more benefits' that they might be interested in. If you have done your job well, these extra benefits would have already arisen in the conversation - has it is, they didn't, so leave them out - just because you perceive them as benefits - the customer may not - everyone is different.

The final part of closing the sale is the most important part of the entire process - miss this step and all your preparation and hard work will go down the drain.

This is the part where you have to firmly, but politely suggest the way forward/a commitment: whether that be asking for an order, proposing a next appointment or agreeing that you put a proposal together.

The way you do this depends upon what you are asking the customer to do. But, as in most things with sales it is best just to say it in the simplest way you can, such as:

"If you are happy with what we've discussed today, would you like to go ahead?"

You will note that this is a simple, almost casual closed question.

If you have done your job well the answer is likely to be Yes. If so, make the next appointment, draw up a proposal, take the order etc.

If it's a No, you may have missed something, and you will probably have to start questioning again... until you discover the missed problem or need. When you have found it you will need to go back to the close.

Once you have closed the call, you need to close the meeting simply and professionally. If it's gone well let the customer know you are pleased, but don't go over the top - shake hands, thank them for their time and leave.

Golden Rule #12: Never argue with a customer

If it didn't go well, a similar process, thank the customer warmly for their time, shake hands and leave. Always leave the customer feeling pleased to have met you, whether you have achieved your goal on this visit or not - this is vitally important for your credibility when revisiting this customer at a later date or for informal third party references from this person (that is, if he mentions you to his peer group, work colleagues etc. you want it to be in a positive light, after all they may be prospective customers).

Epilogue, the Follow-Up

Immediately after the call a good salesperson will perform, what I call, simple self-coaching (or post call self-analysis). Take a piece of paper or a page in the back of your diary. And write down:

What did I do well in the call?

What could I have done better?

What I will do differently next time?

A lot of salespeople miss this step, and simply get into their car and drive off, others find this type of self-analysis uncomfortable (after all, if they do it honestly, it may unearth some areas of behavior or planning that they need to work on) - these people tell themselves it was a wonderful call (whatever the result) and they too get in the car and drive off.

Super successful salespeople always appraise their own performance post call, because they know that making mistakes is human, and as long as they can recognize them, they can learn from them.

This post call self-coaching is not an excuse to 'beat yourself up', that will make your confidence no good whatsoever and put you in a poor frame of mind for your next call. Accept that whatever happened in the call, good or bad is in the past, so don't dwell on it - after all it cannot be changed. Simply approach this part of the day accepting that nothing is (ever) perfect and there is always something positive to be learned from every experience (always!).

So first of all, give yourself a good 'mental' pat on the back for all the things you did right in the call (these will be fairly evident from the reactions you evoked from your customer), especially make a note of the things you did that really helped build rapport with your customer. Although all customers are different, you can sometimes replicate the good things you did in one call by reproducing them in the next (an obvious one is smiling more - nearly everyone responds favorably to that).

The second part of the analysis calls for you to be very honest with yourself in making a note of what you could have done better. Recognizing where you could have done better is a key characteristic of successful salespeople. You must take the lead in a sales call, so everything that happens in a sales call is essentially your responsibility - this is not an opportunity to blame other things: the bad weather, your grumpy boss or the bad mood the customer was in. All of these outside events or circumstances are outside of your control, but you can choose how you react to them.

You choose your attitude towards everything, it is totally under your control, choose it carefully - and choose to positively learn from any (so-called) mistake you have made during a call.

The last part of the analysis is simply to make a note of the things you will do differently next time, these will obviously feed on from the second section of the analysis (above), take positive steps or actions as soon as possible to ensure that these things are done differently next time. Then do them.

Although the face-to-face sales call is the sharpest tool in any good salesperson's toolbox. Never forget what must be done before the call (preparation). Equally important is what must be done after the call. From the first telephone call or face-to-face sales call the customer will make a connection between you and the product he is buying, or more accurately between you and the company that produces that product.

To the customer you are the company, and whatever you do now, whether perceived as good or bad reflects upon the company.

You now need to take responsibility for any interaction between your company and the customer, although as mentioned in an earlier section, you cannot do everything - your new customer will expect you to sort everything out for them - this you must do to the best of your ability, in reality you are the customer's link to the company, but in the customer's eyes you *are* the company.

This requires some work on your part, but mostly it requires organization and honesty.

Another thing you need to do post sales call is to organize anything you have promised to do for the customer. If you promised to send them a proposal, do it at the first opportunity and get it back to them. If you promised to find the answer to a question from someone else in the organization do it immediately.

You have made a successful call, and both you and the customer are happy with the result, the time immediately after the call is when you can re-enforce your relationship with the customer by making good on your promises quickly and effectively.

Even if you haven't promised the customer any further paperwork it is always best to get back in touch with the customer shortly after the call. If the customer has ordered your product/service give them a call as their delivery is due to ensure they are happy with their purchase. Doing this will raise your credibility even higher with the customer and if they do have some issues with the product/service this will give you an opportunity to resolve them quickly, before a small issue mutates into a big problem.

Lastly, you need to update your customer records (whether the call went well or otherwise). This will be a key requirement of your position, so get into the habit of doing it right away before the details become fuzzy. Keeping good, concise customer records will help you in the long run, and will be useful when analyzing what worked and what didn't. They will also help in formulating a long-term business plan for the customer (assuming they will be a long term customer).

Presentations/Workshops

We've gone through a lot over the last few sections; by now you should be aware of what you need to do before, during and after a sales call. All the examples so far assume that you have had a one-to-one sales meeting, and whilst this is often the case, at some time you will need to follow the Simple Steps to Sales Success for a meeting with a group of people.

Presenting to a group of people follows the same basic principles as presenting one-to-one, there are however some points worth mentioning:

Why are we here?: I know it's 'the' big question and I don't know the answer either, but I do know that you need to make sure the group of people that are in your presentation know why you are there, so ensure you introduce yourself properly, tell them why you are there and give them an idea of what's in it for them.

Positive visualization: Visualization is important when presenting to a group. Visualize yourself presenting your product to the group in the most positive manner possible, this includes visualizing how you will feel when you present to the group (confident, relaxed), how you will stand (relaxed, not always still but not running around either), how you will answer questions (confidently, assured). Visualize a very positive ending (the group applauding, or thanking you for a great presentation and you attaining your goal for the meeting).

Preparation: If you can try to take a look at the room you will be presenting in beforehand, this will help you plan where you put things (flipchart to the right or the left of the room, where are the electrical sockets for the data projector etc.). Seeing the room will also greatly help you in your pre presentation visualization.

A friendly face: It is often helpful to have a 'friend' in the audience to strengthen your case by giving an 'unbiased' 3rd party reference. This can often be a person you have met with previously and already sees the value of your product, in a group of peers, their opinion may count for more than yours; so if they are positive about your product let them add 'weight' to your presentation. If you have a person in mind regarding this, check if it is OK with them beforehand to refer to them in your presentation.

If someone is going to introduce you to the group (e.g. The leader of the group), this can be a very positive thing, and if done well it should impart some credibility immediately to you. Before the introduction, however, make sure that you know exactly what they are going to say and that it is line with what you are going to say - otherwise you could end up with a confused audience.

Interruptions and Talkers: A large group of people is generally much harder to manage than a one-to-one meeting. Within every large group you may find some disruptive influences, and these need to be handled with care. Generally these tend to fall into two categories, the first being interruptions, this can take the form of a 'heckler' or a person that simply 'hogs' the attention by asking constant questions often going off on tangents which disrupt your flow and does not allow anyone else to ask questions. Often these people like attention, and one of the easiest things to do is to give it to them, this might be a simply asking them to be a model (if for example you wear your product), this will give them the attention they need, but you can keep them close and under control - they are less likely to be disruptive if they are right next to you. Talking is the other main interruption, this is not generally aimed at you, but occasionally you will find some 'chatterbox' at the back talking all the way through your presentation. There are a couple of ways you might handle this, the first and probably the best is for you to simply stop talking, everyone else will also go quiet, then your 'chatterbox' will realize that they are the only ones talking and everyone is 'waiting' for them and promptly stop. If this doesn't work, directly ask them if they have got a question - this usually cools them down.

Awkward questions: The rule with questions in any sales call, including group presentations is to be honest. Don't make things up, you will be caught out in the end and your reputation will suffer. If you don't know the answer to a question (and this will often happen), acknowledge that it's a good and valid question, tell them you don't know the answer, then tell them you will find out the answer as soon as possible (and make sure you do). Another way of dealing with an awkward question is to 'bounce it back' either to the person who originally asked it by paraphrasing it ("... so what you are asking is...?") or to the audience in general ("That's a good question, does anyone one else have an opinion on that?). Bouncing it back tends to either diffuse the question, or more often than not the person who asked it or the audience will end up answering it!

The Way Forward

The simple guidelines set down in this book are easy to follow - if you want to - but you must want to! To be a successful salesperson (or successful in anything for that matter) you need to stand out from the crowd. This is easier than you think and following the Simple Steps to Sales Success will help you get there faster.

Work is required when reaching for something worthwhile, which is what makes it worthwhile. How many people have you spoken to throughout your life who have succumbed to a work life of mediocrity; they get a job, buy a house, pay the mortgage and hang on to job they don't particularly like because they feel that it is the lifeboat that keeps their world afloat (house, mortgage, car etc.)?

They are the majority, they are the crowd.

It doesn't have to be that way; a sales career offers the opportunity to grow your annual earnings, but more importantly your pride in your chosen vocation.

All you need is a little bit of discipline and the Simple Steps to Sales Success - follow them and you will soon be standing out from the crowd - and once that happens... you will never go back.

Golden Rule #13: Have fun!

A Special Offer!

This guide is based on my Premium Udemy online course 'Keep It Simple Sales Skills: Selling the Easy Way'.

The course covers, in detail, the simple and effective strategies to sell more, with integrity, honesty and trust. It also includes all future updates and my personal help through the Udemy messaging system.

If you use the code below to enroll in the 'Keep It Simple Sales Skills: Selling the Easy Way' course, you can get the entire course for just $20 (normally $99), and as a bonus, you will also get access to a special link within the course so you can get the 'Get a Job in Sales: Your Fast Track to Success' course as well absolutely free.

Go to: www.udemy.com/the-keep-it-simple-sales-course-sell-the-easy-way/ , click on **'redeem a coupon'** and enter the the following code: **KISSSEB20**

To your future sales success!

If you have enjoyed this book and found it useful, it would be great if you could kindly leave a review? I would very much appreciate it!

Thank you and good luck.

And finally...

A big thank you for choosing to buy this guide. I hope you enjoyed reading it as much as I enjoyed writing it!

I would really appreciate it if you could take the time to write a short review on Amazon or whichever marketplace you purchased it from and tell me and other readers interested in the same subject what you thought of the guide. For example, what it was you liked about the guide and if there is anything to improve it further or indeed any ideas for follow up guides. It takes no time at all to write a quick review and it will help other ambitious people decide if this is the product for them.

You really need to give yourself a huge pat on the back for taking action and reading this guide, most people are dreamers... not you.

You have taken an important step in achieving the success you want.

Best Wishes,

Steve Atkinson